A Wee Wur Wi' a Pe

By Anna Pritchard

Table of Contents

Dedication

To my much loved children Lindsay, Lucy and Ross— and to my grandchildren Saskia ,Callum, Imogen and Alia

Acknowledgement

I would like to thank Harry Langham at Goldsters who has been a huge inspiration, and also all my fellow poets from all over Britain who meet on Fridays at our machines.We give each other a lot of positive feedback.

About the Author

I have had a busy life as a mother and teacher, but now have time to think about what I want to say.I am mad about singing and left London twenty two years ago after thirty eight years to settle in the West Country.I am, inspired by my beautiful surroundings and can see Wales across the Bristol Channel from my window.I still feel very Scottish however and this makes me a little rootless.

A Curse

You who are always afraid
I hope that you will meet strange alien creatures
Who look different
Who do things you never do
Who tell you what they are really thinking
Who try to change things
I hope that you will never feel confident
With your classic clothes, standard haircuts ,average accents, nice cars,
two point four children, curries, but always the same ones, constant
politeness, never saying what you think
I am actually afraid of you
Smothered by your acceptance and inertia,
I hide my true feelings
Just to survive
I know that you have always affected my life
adversely by your lack of ambition and understanding
In this democracy that isn't
I wish for you
To watch me and people like me
Get what they want for once
Light, colour, truth in our world

A Love Poem to my Choirs

During the lockdown, we used zoom to keep singing together, though we couldn't hear each other.

I miss you, miss you in my quiet moments
The proximity of sound
That seems to enter me
I am enclosed here in this body, in this mind
The curtains and the dark
My accomplices in solitude
Listening to the rhythms and flights
I have that facility
With my machines
I am waiting here in the dark to emerge
Like a chrysalis
My voice joining you all
Faces becoming solid
Sound waves mixing
I cannot wait
But one day
Maybe soon
And for now
The sound of my own voice
Breaks the silence of my cell

A Room in Someone's House

There always seemed to be onions
It seemed they'd just been fried
There was a feeling of closeness
And a fear of contamination
The walls coated with years of grease
Seemed to be closing in
As if you needed protective clothing
There was a faint echo of jazz
Coming from the next room
And then he was there
His voice in my ear
Claxon like Cockney tones
He was wearing that funny little hat
He'd picked up in Bali
Glaring and blaring colours
Assaulting my senses
With the smell and stickiness
I fought my desire to have a shower
And readied myself to eat
Whatever delicious concoction
He was preparing
Wishing I had stayed outside
With the lovely soothing jazz
On his floor cushion
Which reminded me of my youth

An Attempt at a Sonnet

The April days have not been flush with rain
The sun is streaking down the sprouting leaves
This is the time to wander down the lane
And hope the warmth can overcome the breeze

I never thought the sun would come again
But who can say exactly how it goes
Either it rains and pours and then
We wait until our garden grows

Or we give up and go to somewhere else
But I am tired of always moving on
The Earth no longer weaves in me its spells
I want to be at home among my own

The trouble is I don't know how to tell
The place I feel my seeds were sown

A Spooky Poem

You called me this morning
Your beautiful ears and your fluffy tail
I cannot wait to put you on my pillow
Will you be in my dreams
Silently shadowing my inner heart
With your bouncy blue knitted body?
I will not think of your secret wishes
I will sail through the sea of my sleep
Not hearing your strange rumblings
As you hover above my bed
Taking my breath in one puff
Away you will fly to a new world
And I will be left with wide open eyes
And a gaping mouth
To leave the witnesses puzzled beyond life
As to my sudden departure from it all

Advice

I used to complain about not having a social life
My days were filled up with necessary trivia
Just cooking ,caring, everyday living
And then you were gone
I felt so alone
It was me- always me-or nothing
I remembered your advice
You need to cultivate your friends
Not easy for me
But I started-slowly- a few phone calls-arrangements
The secret seemed to be
Thinking about others
How were they?
Did they need something from me?
And yes, Sometimes that worked
It took me years
The things that seemed easy for you
For me were difficult to do
I put aside my fears, trusted in myself
Knowing there was no-one else
Your advice was the best I could have had
And it turned out not so bad.

After Prufrock

I have measured out my life in;
Dry mouths, stuffed sinuses, sweat, reluctant awakenings, rain, wind,
boredom, time off, sunshine, children, people at bus stops, hoovering,
animals, cooking for every day, cups of tea, biscuits, glasses of wine,
washing and ironing, soap operas, films, music, singing, dancing,
writing, moving around,
But not coffee spoons

All in a Day

This is the beginning
A bird sings
The drunk cradles his hangover
Shop blinds are raised
Trams clank on metal
A figure stands at a bus stop
An urgent call of nature
Steaming piss
A baby cries
Coughs and splutters of a smoker
Unsteady staggers
Black holes under eyes
Coffee

This is the middle
Sun is relentless
Under the canopies
Huge noise, laughter, shouting
Clatter of plates
Smell of fish, garlic,roast meat
Waiters rush around
Sweat dripping off their faces
People sit alone with newspapers
Sinking into a torpor
Renewing themselves
To face the street again

This is the end
Violet sky
Quietness
Twinkling of lamps
Down the hill
A Sliver of a breeze
Stirs the tablecloths

Still fluttering
Faint sound of singing
Floats up
There is brandy on the table

12

Amelia

In 1975
Amelia
So cool
So good-looking
She cycled along Euston Road to get to college
For me
The bravest thing
In love with music
She sang in Velvet Fist
We both did sociology
As part of our B.Ed
On a weekend
Like being at school
Sharing a room
We smoked Amelia's dope
Played Cheat
With all the others
Laughing hysterically
Mature students?
Outside we had a life
She literally tore her hair out
Before the exams
Later we stayed in touch
In overlapping social circles
Through all the twists and turns
Of relationships
Our children grew up
And there was the Mill
A hub, a meeting place
When I was isolated and alone
She always remembered me
She phoned
Her friendship so valuable
Not hearing her

Not sharing stories
Unthinkable,unbelievable
Amelia with her guitar in the Mill
Singing the songs in her battered notebooks
That I began to know
We hoped to sing together at Burns night
She always put herself second
But she should have been first.

Audrey Hepburn Wakes Up
Confused in a Glasgow Nightclub

Oh dear! I wish I hadn't tried that third single malt
I couldn't get over the cold and damp
My little black dress is really not suitable

But he's such a sweetie
When I understand him
Aghh the taste in my mouth
They should never have let him look after me

I can't believe they think that's jazz
What are they saying?
If you don't listen hard
It sounds so low and angry
Like thunder rumbling under your feet

What do I do now?
Can you hear me?
I'm talking to you

No dear, I'm waiting for someone
No, I don't want another drink

If only it wasn't so cold outside
I'd just go and get a taxi

Another New Year

This will be my seventy ninth
Swishing in
Memories
Rags stuffed into a pillowcase
Which refuses to contain them
Incomprehensible and embarrassing personal bits
Spilling out rebelliously
I cannot gather them together
Edit, make sense, choices impossible
Our old house
Stale cigarette smoke, empty glasses
Comatose figures
Singing so much your voice dried up
The warmth of others
Now gone into emptiness
Leaving
A scrambled heap
Fragments
Accumulating in the tight packed frenzy of my psyche

Ansaphone

Hello,hello(sung)
I'm not here
I'm out having a great time
But I'm always happy to hear from you
If you need me
Keep trying
If you want to sell me something
Don't bother
What is that Beatles song?
Hello hello I don't know why you say goodbye I say hello(sung)
Ciao

Baroque

Curlicues, nymphs, cherubs
Wigs and brocade breeches
Columns and arches
The places they went
To get their culture
Foreign lands
Where they found paintings, pottery, fabrics
Spinets and clavichords
Tinkling and precise
Serried formations
The coming and going
Of minuets and country dances
Arrogantly displaying
Excesses of ornamentation
Reminds me of my
four-year-old desire for party frocks
Frills and furbelows
The candy floss of all our histories

Bed Time

They have gone
To whirl in the unnamed territory
Of their soothed sweeping blankets
To huddle their softness in a warm womb

And their heads are marble
Like ancient majestic cherubs
The classic pose of repose

They will swing up the eddies of their minds
Under cover of the dark subconscious
And they will echo
The reverberations
Of the dead day

In the end a beginning
The discarded shroud of sleep
Floating unnoticed to the floor
As they rise with clear eyes of hope
To eat their cornflakes

Bertie

Bertie! Your wise face
Untroubled
Your warmth given
You took what you needed
You gave back double
Meeting the cars
Like a faithful lover
You were there
And there you will stay
In our hearts

20

Burns Night

After New Year
The days short and sad
I look towards Burns night
To make my heart glad
Haggis ,neeps and tatties
I used to make the soup
The songs and the practise
To keep me in the loop
We started full of promise
With whisky on the table
To go through the process
Of becoming more unstable
Finally I found myself
Frenzied participation
Jumping up and singing
Without any hesitation
The mouthy and the guitar(mouth organ)
And someone on the spoons
Singing from my crazy heart
Whatever made me start
Tomorrow I will croak
And others will joke
About my bad behaviour
But I will not care

Customs

Angst beset us
Dark mornings, slow to light
Moving towards longer days
The strained voice of my mother
She cleaned and scoured
Blackbun cooked, windows washed, cupboards cleaned
Frenzy of movement, urgency of provision
Off-licences queued out, whisky got in
She made me ginger wine for my bottle
Non alcoholic
I was allowed to stay up till the bells
The table laid with perfect lace tablecloth
Fire raked out and reset
Freshly washed and dressed up
Salmon sandwiches
Home made shortbread
Christmas cake
Then the ritual
Precision of the hour
Raised glasses
Waiting for the first foot
Hoping for a tall dark man
To bring us luck for the year
Where did all that come from?
Was it the Celts?
Who knows
But to start afresh is good

Disappearance

He disappeared in the dead of winter
He said he was just going out for a while
It was easy to understand
Claustrophobic didn't say it well enough
We tried to keep our spirits up
He taught me how to play scrabble
Always the trickster
I thought it was about words
He was all about tactics
I was glad for a while
I could just have sandwiches
Cooking had been a chore
And why was it always my chore?
It was cold in bed
I started wearing socks
Then the strange phone calls started
I tried not answering
But it could have been him
He was the one with the friends
I had none
I thought about looking for him
But he had to have a place to come back to
Sometimes I thought I heard his key in the lock
And then panicked – was it a stranger?
Its spring now. The daffodils he planted are out.
Wisps of sun are creeping through
I don't cry
What's the point?
I just have an empty feeling.

For You

Sometimes you just pop up
It's always when I'm not consciously
Thinking of you
Or maybe in a dream
My God it's twenty years
But you remain a part of me
There's a lot of anger still
But not enough to ruin my life
There's also the little things
Like the crazy stories you used to tell
How I envied you that ability
To make something ordinary remarkable
Other people important to you are dying now
And I wonder
What you would have said at their funerals
Would you get the technology?
And would I get anywhere near a laptop
If you were around?
I believed I knew what you were thinking
But I probably didn't
Such a different world now
But I'd love to discuss it with you
You'd laugh and be horrified with me I think
I eat mussels sometimes and think of you

Fragments

Bloom
Blossom
Lower arch
Several branches
A stray wisp of movement
The echo of quietness
Moving into shade
Then straightening
A solid round
Firmly stood
With strength
Rooted
Under
Earth

Hello everybody,
Lovely to see you
This is a complex brain
Don't jump too fast
Things will unravel
As we travel
Just here at the frontal lobe
Is the reasoning part
Not always functioning

From a Hearing of Capricho Arabe

I am dancing
Tangoing
My heart is lifting and lilting
I feel warmth in my body
Like a beautiful sherry
moving through
A continuity in the repetition
But the lilting is hard
To resist
I want to move
In a long rivering movement
In the arms of music
And back
Down a sunlit valley
Trees intercepting sun
And I want it to go on
It soothes
Like a warm wrapping
It leaves the grey behind
Long behind
My soul needs this
The rays of that world
Calling me
With a savour of love
And satisfaction

Going Home

He came home, said nothing
I took the dish of dried up stew
And put it down
He looked at me in perfect innocence
I waited
He said nothing
I went upstairs and read
But I was angry
I went back
He said nothing
I packed my bags and called a cab
He said nothing
I went to my mother's house
I cried
But said nothing

Haunted Ruin

I started in sunlight
A simple ruin
After claustrophobia
A breezy jaunt
Just putting one foot before the other
But ,as the chill began to seep into my core,
I felt the darkening as a shiver
Then came that roosting call
A frenzy of birds
Seeking safety
I wondered
About the lives
Of the long dead
In this space
Horses shuffling in their stalls
Rattle of their harnesses
Last flickering of kitchen fires
Mice dancing round walls
Snoring figures
In the strawstrewn hall
Schemers through shadows
Slinking with shaded candles
Lovers doing what they do
Assassins intent
And I felt afraid

His Happy Place

Walking in
Fug and mist
Gone now
Not allowed
Lively buzz
Animated talk
Three figures at a table
Caught in time
Slow motion
Not always silent
Heads down
Intent
Crosswords
Quick consultations
Gaps of contemplative silence
Comings and goings
Rounds to be bought
Each new arrival
Acknowledging his presiding
His stories
Banal but funny
Timing and absurdity
Enhancing them
His embroidery of the facts
My torment resisting
The contradictions I swallowed
An everyday ritual
Tedious for me
His happy place

I Am Not Angry

I am not angry that the buses in my town only run when drivers turn up
I have stopped using them
I go nowhere
I am not angry that there is now no post office
I don't send mail anymore
I am not angry that getting to see a doctor is almost impossible
I content myself with the thought that I don't really matter very much
I try not to get ill
I am not angry that there are no trains
I just avoid travelling
I am not angry that all the normal necessities have doubled in price
I just eat less
I am not angry that I have to think about it every time I turn on the heating
I just stay in bed-- or wrap blankets round me
I am not angry that my assets, such as they were, are worth a lot less than they used to be worth
I won't be needing them where I am going
I am not angry
I am incandescent with rage

Imogen's Granny

When you come out of school today
Open your eyes
You will see me
I am your Granny
And I make you pancakes
Every day at half past three
The school comes out
And here I am
Always by the roundabout
I check your coat
And tie your scarf
And then I try to make you laugh

We wander home
Through rain flecked streets
And in we go
To get our treats
For me it's tea
For you it's cocoa
And pancakes always there to follow

In Media Res

We are milling
Happily turning over
Our new hairdos, and dramatic news
Or just sadness
Reds weaving in and out
Winding and waving
Tee shirs with vibe
Then a call to
GATHER
And warm up
A sudden formation
Getting muscles and voices ready
Strange sounds
Yawning and stretching
Rhythmic chants and voices
Wisping and whispering
Into the wild roar
Of the wind
But then
The singing started
We listened to each other
Our own voices like peeled grapes
Popping out of their long taut skin
Rejoicing in each other

Land Links

The colours of this land
Are light and striking
The beach eternally pleasant
There are a few trees
Urgently needed for shade
When the soles of feet are scalded
And the rhythmic swishing
of the tide cradling your mind
Into a hypnotic trance
It is a world of delight
At the fringes of the land
There are stony paths going down
And you imagine the small town
Which once nestled there
On the Libyan sea
In the archeological site along the beach
They have uncovered the traces
of great harbours and temples which they think were landing places
Of Egyptians, Phoenicians,Greeks,Minoans
and other travellers.
They say the rubbish dump held bones, mussel shells, pottery
You can imagine boats landing
with slaves, pottery ,minerals and other things
Feasting on the beach
Commerce from all over the Mediterranean
"They loved to party"
said the archeologist who showed us round
Who wouldn't party in this place?
We remember the long road of humankind
Living under the same blue skies
And enjoy the lasting presence
of these distant travellers and local people
Who looked and lived like us

Last Night It Startled Me Again

From a Line from Dirt and Light as Published in the New Yorker

Last night it startled me again
The memory
Your sense, your smell
Your warmth
I was overwhelmed
Conflicted
Fearful even
This presence
Unfathomable
As we struggled with the information
You stayed with me all day
The child somersaulting in my belly
I did not believe in this
But I knew what I felt
Fifty years or more
And I still remember
My sense of the loss of you
So long ago
My necessary
Rationalisation

Lilac Sky

Cool evening
Raucous boys on bikes
Evening shopping
I am seated in my best bar
My ritual pre-prandial ouzo in front of me
People still coming back from the beach
Sweaty and dishevelled
Showered and dressed for the evening
I watch the sky
It fades very slowly
To pink, to lilac ,to purple
The bustle starts to slow
Movements become less frequent
A hush falls
I greet the occasional passer-by
The sky darkens imperceptively
Suddenly it's dark
Time to make a decision
Where to eat tonight?
(this is probably my most loved place, a village in Crete)

Message

Open me when you need me most
I am not really like your normal post
I am the magic that goes inside your head
Seeks out and destroys the lurking pest
I go like some robot deputed to clean
The hoover that randomly cleans the whole scene
I smell and trace the paranoia
That blooms inside like a flower
A weed really!
These evil thoughts that take away your peace
And niggle without a timely release
They lurk inside in spite of all attempts
To stick to rationale and sense
You will not find me wanting
Through conditions quite daunting

Mevagissey

Crowds revolving
Gawping and guzzling
Pasties, fish and chips

Queues
Seagulls
Ravished calls
Food craving shadows
Always on the look out

Echoing
Harbour
Sea smells
Crabbing, paddling, climbing
Dogs and kids happy
Nostalgic

Sunshine
Showers later
Clothes in layers
British weather
Dampness

Moods

Crying comes easily nowadays
I really can't tell what starts it

Memories leave a slippery trace
Like a slug's spit
On a dark tile

When a new day is freshly lit
The sun makes me stop awhile
Shadows vanish, glare blots out
The deepest wrinkles of my smile

And now it's time to dance and shout
Sing with every breath that comes
Celebrate the world about
The sounds that guide your feet
Are echoing your own heartbeat

Mothering

At that apocalyptic time
In my vast roundness
Inside me
Eight months of cocooned life
You, the strongest, suddenly bereft
A little dried up bird
Corrupted by shock
Shrunken and shrivelled
I had to hold you
My swelling absorbing your shrinkage
Onion shelling
Skin over skin
We clung together
You carried on shaking
I could not undertake
The new mothering
I needed for you
The all knowing one
But so it was
I did my best
And slowly you began
To fluff your wings
Regaining serenity
Your motherhood long established
With mine still finding its way
And still renewing every day

Not Taking Myself Too Seriously

How many mince pies can you eat
Before it becomes less than a treat
My legs are frozen solid
From standing singing horrid
songs about bells
How many ding dongs can you. sing
Before you start to hate everything
about Christmas
Sorry,sorry
I know I'm supposed to be jolly
I am forced to overindulge
In all things causing a bulge
In my already too big belly
Thank God it's nearly over
And I can get back to my usual moaning
About the state of everything

November

November
The sun is glinting sharp
No longer hidden by leaves
Tree's black limbs
Letting in the light
Bursts of precious pleasure
Among the damp stodge
A spot of honeydew
Rain and wind
Creeping under the cover
Of my layers of wrapping
Frisking my flapping scarf
In a cold shower of reality
No more sunbathing for a while.

Ode to Slade Road

The mornings are special
The soft summer air blanketing me
I walk to the corner
Turn right
The bit I know
The first half
A sloping garden
Straying flowers
Escaped somehow from beds
Listen--- Almost silence
Further along
Our local celebrities
Wallace and Gromit
Sean the sheep
Linger in one garden
Sometimes there are people
But mostly not
I try not to hurry
And remind myself
To drink in the drowsy smugness
Of this lush green road
Which always fills my heart
With serenity, as well as pleasure.

On Not Fitting In

When I cannot feel what others do
I wonder if it's me or you
I chose to be here
No-one made me come
But sometimes it's clear
That this is not my home
The anger that I sometimes feel
Allows me to know something real
Although I try to hide it well
My nearest ones can always tell
But what else is there?
A world I left behind
To navigate new paths
And open up my mind
It was not easy
But happened in the end
Dancing and manoeuvering
To know who was my friend
So
Here I am
Here I will stay

This is dedicated to the people of Ukraine, also the young Russian men who are unwillingly sent into a war they didn't choose.

On the Front

In the sound drenched outpost
He thought of years past
A fig
Summer luxury
Fallen from dried up branches
Blistered legs leaving
The speckled scars of a life
Full of questions
What else follows
The thread of uncertainty
Except a life
Hoping without confidence
For another sunrise

Outside My Window

Tenacious orange leaves cling to the last tree
Always the last to let go and the last to be renewed
The winter lace has come everywhere else
The sky opaque with folds of filtered light
Serenity, hardly a quiver, after days of violent agitation
My heart doesn't race with the wind today
A bird has discovered my feeder
And now a blackbird, but it doesn't work for him
He can't get in.How does that happen?
I am grabbing time from all the singing occasions
To stop and contemplate the world outside my window
I am almost overcome with the peace
A moment of renewal refilling my consciousness
I know the world around is getting scarier again
But——- the life that goes on renewing itself year after year
In the face of all our anxieties
Continues.

Procrastination

Put away last night's glass
The bathroom needs a clean
That letter about my bus pass
My slippers have gone green
I really need a haircut
I must give Chris a call
The freezer needs defrosting
Tomorrow I'll do it all
That will be the day
When nothing's in the way
Of the tomorrow that's nearly today
The important day

Reflection on the Journey of the Magi

by T.S Elliot

I never thought I would get mixed up in anything like that
Me- always casual, unfussy, comfortable
I couldn't stop myself
I was drawn to it
I became a part of it

Shepherds and important looking strangers
What were they doing there?
Seeing a couple in the shed,
Imagining their journey

What was she to do in her hour of delivery?
What kind of a world is this
When people have to travel with nothing
And drop their babies anywhere?

They were so quiet
Even the animals behind her were quiet
I thought of my own comfortable bed
My healthy children who were always safe
I went away feeling strange
I didn't know what to think

Resignation Letter

It is with deep regret

That I inform you
That I won't be caring any more
I really wish I could continue to cope
But really I can't hold on to reality
I am on a slippery slope

The absurdity of daily life
Has reduced me to a state of incredulity
I shall just hope to get by
I shall sing and write poetry
I shall wear purple and that sort of thing
It's not in my brief
YOU can try
I've watched
The headlong road to destruction
Long enough
I am resigning from the smooth
And the rough
Just let me go
I know you will

This was written when I had been reduced to despair by the political situation

Clerihew

Tony Blair
Looked like a man to care
But his "weapons of mass destruction"
Put an end to his production

Sambucca di Sicilia (Harry's story)

That morning the smell of coffee
Still lingering and the mezzalunas
Still fresh in my mouth
I met a wandering poet
We exchanged names
And ideas. The wanderer
Who somehow sold himself
A jobbing poet
Was an inspiration
How brave
To take one's head and heart
And lay them out on the pavement
For all to see
No tools but pen and paper
What streams played
Into his creative channels?
What stories did he tell?
His material
people around him
Delving and sharing
Open faces or
Ravines of pain and insecurity
And after
Precious paper in little boxes
Or floating away
Ephemera
Swallowed up by an uncaring world

Screens or Screams

There was nothing in my writing that I could call exciting.
But it made me remember
The process of tethering thoughts together
In the face of impervious machines
Automatic takes me on another train
Outside my brain
Can I adapt my formless thoughts
To fit the basic dots
Of metal things
That cling together
In a way that baffles me.
Or must I endlessly struggle
In my own safe muddle
Against the cold hard reality
Of the mechanical world
I have been doing computer acrobatics

Silkie

He came to me at twilight
The orange of the setting sun
Silhouetting his stout frame
When I saw him close
His eyes were luminescent green
Like the swirling sea
I never feared him
His hands were cool on me
His voice made tears
Pour from me
My throat moving up to my mouth
At the depth and roundness
Of his song
He touched my hair
And it ran in ringlets
I felt myself float
In the calm pool by the beach
His arms took me on a rhythmic dance
Softly flowing
From me to him
By morning he was gone
Dissolved into the thick mist
Of forgetfulness

Simple Pleasures

I see the bench empty
I sink in
With gratitude
My tired legs and back
Thank me
I take a deep breath
And sigh
A seagull hovers
Again
But he soon goes
I am not eating
The sun comes out
I hold my face up
I watch the people pass
It's good to be out
In a world that has others in it.

Singing Live Again

At the beginning of the relaxation, we were allowed to sing outside two feet distance from each other. This is about singing live again.

Sunshine sultry in stone
Echoing stepping ground of school playground
We wound around wishing ourselves together,
But two feet apart
Then we made a sizzling sound
Rhythmically ranting in round
Waves washing our voices and winding words together
Melodies and mimes mixing
Bodies bending and air bouncing in our bucking lungs
Singing, singing---
Sounding the suppressed sobs and sighs of the last terrible times
Maybe over, let's hope

The Song of the Sofa

I am
That old thing
By the back door
Shabby from dead cats' claws
Covered in bright cotton
For sitting on
To bathe in the rare sunshine

From the wide window
Lately she lies on me
Covered with a heavy blanket
Enveloping herself in my warmth
Lying horizontally
Limbs and flesh
Watching a screen flicker and shadow
Arms behind her head
Sometimes asleep
Then shouting and swearing

Getting back on her feet
She does strange rocking movements
It's a completion when she lies on me
Before I was just here doing nothing

Sorry I Forgot the Name of this Beautiful Piece of Music

Let me flow forever onwards in your dancing arms
I see your hand touching the strings and stretching my unconscious voice
Slathering me in waves of melody like a beautiful soft tongue
You are pulling me and pulling me
My very innards are jumping and heaving at every stroke
Horizons new
Looking out to a new pinkness
The sun billows out
As the birds hover about and continuously demand
Legions of feathery trees extending to the endless road
A new place beyond
It is changing
I hear the end coming
Suddenness
Still again
Heartstrings cry

Storm

Trees like banshees
Water in strange places
Stay in and keep warm
The pulse races
In another form
Inserting my world
In the home's embraces
As we did before
Except the drama is visible
The howling audible
There is only the waiting
With hope for the abating

Summer

Strawberries are like a shout
Unavoidable
Rituals involving their innards
Reminds me of my mother
Always fearing the worlds worst
Outcomes
The coiled worm
At the heart
They are fantastic
I'll take them
Smidgeoned with sugar
And fresh podded peas
Reminding me of my granny
Who put them into broth
If I had some left
From the empty pods

Heaped at my front
It rained a lot
Trips out were often
Tales of woe
Sodden sandwiches
And communal races
In sopping fields
Under dripping trees

But later
The discovery of
Exciting horizons
Delight of foreign voices
Soft and extravagant heat
Which drowned me
In its embrace

Happy exhaustion
Nothing to do
But read and talk
Nights of singing and exuberance
Go hang with your hangovers
You can stay in bed tomorrow
If that is your desire
An escape from all the grey
From every day
THAT was the summer.

Thankyou

For being there
When I came
I was afraid, shy, insecure
You let me be me
You let me try shakily
To sing. I loved it.
I still felt afraid and unsure
But there were always the voices around me.
I listened
I learned
The songs moved my soul
I listened to myself
I learned from you
The breathing
The pitfall of S
The cut off and timing
All of this
From you
More and more
I became a different person
With a life worth living
Belief in myself
The music is still my lifeline
I owe it all to you
You changed my life.

That Tree

That tree fills my window
I can see its grey and green solidity
Starting with a foot planted into the green
Splayed segments like chunky toes
The trunk uniform and straight
The branches combing out into feathery lace
Without leaves now it is stark
Behind it blue fades into a grey sky
Yellow luminosity down against the triangles of roofs
Washing light upwards
Dominating the view and defining the season
Soft buds, abundant greenery and decadent warmth of autumn
Or now, when it shows the emptiness of of winter
Contrasting thick branches with elegant tracery of twigs
Hinting at the promise of new beginnings

The Fall of Icarus

What was that splash out there?
It hardly sounded
A faint plop
Inside my ear
A Cretan landscape
So dear as always
The curves and terraces
Made by a plough
The shepherd with his whistle
Jangles of sheep
The remote signs of civilisation
Shimmering in the broiling sun
The fishermen intent on today's catch
Life and commerce
In full flow
But-- was there something
A tic in the throat,
A foot crack in the forest?
As I, in my cave
think
Is it entirely gone?
That surge of audacity
That need for height
Reaching, reaching
Sun, oh life giver and destroyer
Let me go
Yes -- I let you go

The Moon

That sense of wonder
Darkness illuminated
Another world
Inhabited in wild moments
I sense a hysteria
Observed from a distance
Detached from the everyday
Think of lovers
And plotters in the shadows
It fills an indefinable emptiness in me
Mountains, warmth
The scent of vegetation
Sage and Thyme
Quiet
Wolves howling
Why do they do that?
Do they feel that wonder and longing?
The werewolf in me
Hiding in suburbia
Unleashing who knows what devastation

These Words

These words are meant to be learned before the concert
Needing my brain to be fully alert
Hanging in my mind like discarded litter
Not making enough sense to be in my transmitter

These words are going to bed to call me up in the night
Causing nightmares to get them right
Not giving me any inspiration
Filling me with desperation

These words are finally going in there if it kills
Repeat, repeat until my head fills
With words that finally fit together
And bring me back from the end of my tether

Transition

Do nothing
Wait a year
You need to grieve
After a year
House in sad decline
I wanted out
I went to Bristol
New life, new identity
New house
A delight
I could do what I liked
I knew no-one in the whole city
That sense of isolation
I will never forget
Going out, just to go out
Knowing you will not meet anyone
I thought I had become mad and sad
Through some fault of mine

No-one could help me
It's over now
I have a new life
I know lots of people
I have a new identity
I am me.

Underdog

I watched the dramas
Of the dogs in the village
Their ribs protruding over taut bellies
The bitch on heat
Pursued by rabbles of assorted mongrels
Never given peace
For once she had attention
I saw the swaggering pets
Paraded in all their glory
While snivelling ,starving shadows
Skulked around the narrow echoing streets
Howls and growls
Nighttime skirmishes
The soft brush of warm flesh on one's thigh
The hopeful and doleful eyes
As you chewed on your juicy pork chop
It wasn't hard to imagine
The life of an underdog

What is a Poem?

is the skip in a hop ,skip and jump
takes you on a leap of faith
stirs the syrup in your innards
lifts you out of the doldrums
pushes you to reflect
makes your heart sing
stops you in your prosaic tracks
brings tears
makes you use your voice
repeats in your head
wakes you in. the dead of night
soothes your frenzy
brings a sigh from you
gives you strength
paints the world
sings the universe
perfumes the empty day
gives peace
answers your anger

What is Being Human

What is being human
And how do I describe it?
Hot blood runs through me
I feel pain and pleasure
What's that? you say
Strengthening its enormity
My heart feels good
It's happiness- yes
But what is that?
I cry when I'm in pain
That's when my body tells me
It's not happy
Or if a loved one is in pain
Tears come from my eyes
Love, you say, what's that?
How can I tell you?
Put your arms around me
Feel my warmth, listen to my heartbeat
Smell me. You don't feel it?
That's so sad
Listen , hear my breath, feel it on you
Let me sing to you
Let your heartbeat tell you to move
Its rhythm will teach you
Dance, speak, delight in language
That is human,Passion is human
I am sorry if you can't have it

Windows

Funnily enough I just got a new set of windows.
It's strange what all this entails.
In my kitchen it involved temporarily removing a table-
and where to put it was difficult.
Now it looks fabulous as I can see the lovely view unimpeded by dried
up -plants and the occasional spider's web or dead fly—a positive
revelation.
In my bedroom it involved moving a bed which was wedged rather
unexpectedly across the narrow width of the room, but, in the process,
I have moved innumerable unworn shoes from one corner to another
and boxes seem to take up less space in their new position.
The dust is much reduced—and I am more sinusally challenged.
Sneezing has become an inveterate activity.
I am very happy.
It looks so clean. I am surprised how quickly I go back to my old ways.
The upheaval is past.

Words

I eat my words
Greedily
I taste them, relish them
They swirl in my mouth
Chocolate or savoury
Foreign, rhythms and reverberations
What a delight are words
When they do not work I am sad
Communication is all
I need them
My words spill out
As half digested guts
Please take them
Understand
I need words

70

9 781916 707160